Smart Clothes

Elizabeth Nonweiler

raintree

tartan kilts

thawb

academic
robe and cap

sari and jewels

matching outfit

white shirt
with necktie

Javanese sarong

shawl

tailcoat

bridesmaid's frock

kente cloth dress

kaftan
made with
cotton
brocade

Interesting facts about the pictures

page 2: **Kilts** are sometimes worn by Scottish or Irish men. They wrap around the waist and are knee length. The pattern is called a tartan. Every Scottish clan (family) has its own tartan.

page 3: A **thawb** is an ankle length robe with long sleeves, often worn by men in Arab countries, especially on important occasions. It is comfortable in the heat because it is white and loose.

page 4: An **academic robe and cap** are worn at a ceremony when a student graduates from university. They show everyone that the student has worked hard and learned a lot.

page 5: A **sari** is a strip of cloth that is wrapped around the body. Saris come from India. On special occasions, ladies wear beautiful jewels with saris. The jewel on this lady's head is a tikka.

page 6: A **matching outfit** like this looks smart for office work. Jackets and trousers or jackets and skirts that match are called suits. A shirt or blouse is worn under the jacket.

page 7: **White shirts with neckties** are often worn by men to look smart at work and on formal occasions. Neckties can have various shapes, knots and names, such as cravats, bandanas and bow ties.

page 8: This Javanese man is wearing a **sarong** for his wedding. It is a length of material that goes around the waist and is folded to hold it in place. Sarongs are worn all over the world.

page 9: A **shawl** is a piece of cloth worn loosely over the shoulders. It is useful for keeping warm, but often it is worn just to look smart and beautiful. This lady is from Thailand.

page 10: A **tailcoat** is a jacket that is long at the back. It was first designed so that a man with a long coat could ride a horse without it getting in the way. Now it is often worn at weddings.

page 11: A **bridesmaid** attends to the bride at her wedding. She is usually a close friend or one of the bride's family. She wears a beautiful **frock** and often carries a bouquet of flowers.

page 12: **Kente cloth** is made by stitching strips of cloth together. There are many patterns and many ways to wrap the cloth around you. It was once worn by kings and queens of Ghana.

page 13: A **kaftan** is a robe with wide sleeves and front opening, often worn by men in West Africa. This one is made with cotton brocade, which means cotton woven with a raised pattern.

Letter-sound correspondences

Level 2 books cover the following letter-sound correspondences.
Letter-sound correspondences highlighted in green can be found in this book.

ant	big	cat	dog	egg	fish	get	hot	it
jet	key	let	man	nut	off	pan	queen	run
sun	tap	up	van	wet	box	yes	zoo	
duck	fish	chips	sing	thin this	keep	look moon	art	corn

say	boy	rain	oil	boat	eat	pie	high
make	these	like	note	flute tube	out	saw	author
her	bird	turn	airport	flew stew	blue cue	phone	when